15 Dogs and a Cat

Speak Out

Interviews by Luke the Detective Dog

Pat McGrath Avery

ISBN soft copy: 978-1-937958-11-4

ISBN ebook: 978-1-937958-01-5

Cover Design and Book Layout:
Joyce Faulkner

Published by Red Engine Press

Contents

Introduction

Hi, I'm Luke the Detective Dog. It's tail-waggin' good to meet you!

Raise your paw if you like dogs!

I bet I'd get a better response if I asked dogs to raise their paws if they like people.

People don't always get it that we make friends just like they do. I decided to do my share for dog-dom. I called on some of my old and new friends asking them to share their thoughts. They all want people to understand dog-thinking (and cat-thinking too) a little better. Come to think of it, I'd like to understand cat thinking.

Dogs and cats come in all shapes, sizes, and colors with much more color and variety than people do. It makes sense that we fascinate people.

One thing all of my four-legged kind share is our love of smell. We have awesome noses and we know how to make the best of them. So I always ask my fellow critters to tell me their favorite smells. If I ever start interviewing people, I'll ask them the same question.

Anyway, once you hear from the dogs (and a cat) in this book, you'll begin to understand what we think about and what's important in our lives.

Happy reading! Oh, and don't forget to hug a dog (and a cat) each and every day! It's healthier than that "apple-a-day" thing. One more piece of advice, when we try to make you laugh doing a bunch of stupid tricks, that's to improve your health and your life. So go ahead and laugh!

Not long ago I met Zoee, a little puppy that will grow up to look like me. I felt it was my duty as a grown-up one-year-old to give a fellow Bichon the wisdom of my experience. Here are my suggestions for puppies who want to make their people happy.

Cuddle up and you will melt your new friend's heart.

The first thing to learn is the potty stuff. People seem to think it's really important.

Your friend's voice will tell you more than his words.

If she tries to teach you to do stuff, learn to do what makes her happiest. My mom taught me how to patty cake. She laughed every time I did it right. It's silly but I patty cake for her every day because I like to hear her laugh.

Don't follow too closely or you'll get stepped on. My mom is kind of a klutz and she steps on me a lot. I've learned to get out of the way really fast.

Play with your food. I don't know why but it makes it taste better.

Don't chase your tail. It's fun but people don't like it.

Share your toys with your friend. She'll think you're adorable.

If you have your own little house, make it comfy. It's your own space. Bury your toys in it but never ever potty in it.

Smile at people and they smile back.

I like people and other dogs. I started thinking that someone needed to find out what we think about things. I made a list of questions and started asking other dogs. I got lots of different answers. Sometimes I changed the questions. Other times, I met dogs that I didn't get a chance to ask them about their lives.

I don't understand cats but I wanted to know more about them. I think the only cat I know really hates me. When we visit his house, he hisses at me. His hair stands up straight and his tail slowly swishes back and forth. He even jumped at me once and scratched my nose with his sharp claws. I just want to be his friend but he sure doesn't want to be mine.

Enough of that. I've interviewed or talked to fourteen dogs and one cat that have expressed their opinions about life and living with people. It's time for people to hear what we really and truly think. So here goes...

🐾

Bella Lund

Figure 1 Bella

Luke: Describe yourself.

Bella: I am a very cute, spoiled, and lovable Yorkie-poo. I am three-years-old and I love to play.

Luke: What is your favorite activity?

Bella: Playing fetch with a stuffed tooth my mom bought for me.

Luke: What is your favorite inside smell?

Bella: Any food my dad is making.

Luke: What is your favorite outdoor smell?

Bella: Goose poop.

Luke: Do you have to do any silly tricks to please your people? If so, what are they?

Bella: Nope.

Luke: What kind of treats do you like?

Bella: Bones from the Meat Market that my Grandma brings me when she visits.

Luke: Do your people share their food with you?

Bella: Sometimes my dad sneaks me some food.

Luke: What are your favorite toys?

Bella: My stuffed tooth, stuffed rabbit and stuffed dog.

Luke: What is your pet peeve? (Now where did that come from?)

Bella: When my brother Buddy tries to eat my food.

Luke: Do you like other dogs?

Bella: It depends how big they are.

Luke: Do you like cats?

Bella: Yes.

Luke: Do you listen when your people tell you to do something?

Bella: If it's my dad, yes....if it's my mom, no....she is kind of a push over.

Luke: Do you have bad hair days?

Bella: Yes.

Luke: Tell me about your family members.

Bella: I love them a lot and they spoil me. I have a brother, Buddy who is a Beagle and another brother Oliver who is a cat and a sister Bailey who is also a cat.

Luke: Is there anything else you'd like to share?

Bella: I love to take showers and baths with my mom...I love the water!!!

My mom even bought me my own armoire for all of my clothes.

Bubba Rodgers

Figure 2 Bubba Rodgers

Bubba, a seven-year-old chocolate Lab, lives in Texas. His mom never wanted a dog in the family but in 2004, her sons took her out to dinner for Mother's Day and convinced her that the whole family needed a puppy.

That's when Bubba became part of the Rodgers family and their lives have never been the same. He easily became the third son to loving parents — isn't that a great dog story?

I asked Bubba to describe himself.

Bubba: I'm a fashion model, long-legged and handsome. Before the other boys left home, I played "buffer" whenever there was family friction. We became a very close family and even though the boys are out on their own now, they still love me.

Luke: What are your favorite smells — outside and indoors?

Bubba: When I'm outside I look for squirrels. They have an awesome smell. In the house, I love the smell of smoked turkey.

Luke: Do you have any favorite toys?

Bubba: Sure. I have a stuffed squeaky snake that I love to toss around. I like Nylabones too.

Luke: Do you like kids and cats?

Bubba: Sure. I'm a social sort of guy. I play super easy with cats, little dogs, and kids. Sometimes they're afraid and I have to remind myself to go easy with them.

Luke: Do you believe in dog heaven?

Bubba: You bet I do. I know I have a soul and if I'm good, I'll go to dog heaven. Mom told me it's a wonderful place with green grass, plenty of trees and flowers, blue skies, and everyone I love.

In my heavenly home, I hope my mom isn't a writer. She needs too much help from me when she's trying to figure out scenes and characters. It's tiring work, plus she talks all the time until I help her solve her problems. She says I'm a good listener.

Luke: Do you like to ride in a car?

Bubba: I love it! When Mom is working, she sometimes takes me for long rides. She's even `named her car the "Bubbamobile" and the "Burban." How cool is that?

The car is the place I help my mom. When it's just the two of us, we can get it done.

Luke: Is there anything else you'd like to tell us?

Bubba: Mom thinks I'm her seven-year-old furry boy and she took my picture when I was wearing a red baseball cap. Dad is a pilot so Mom took a picture of me with goggles. She loves to take pictures and even took me to church to get my picture taken. I guess it's because I'm such a handsome fella.

At night my mom understands what I think when I get in bed with her. Dad's gone a lot. I let Mom know that I love her and I'm glad Dad's flying 'cause she lets me sleep on his pillow. Please don't tell him!

Buddy Lund

Figure 3 Buddy Lund

Luke: Describe yourself.

Buddy: I am a middle aged, mildly overweight, going gray, very lovable and laid back eight-year-old Beagle.

Luke: What is your favorite activity?

Buddy: Sleeping.

Luke: What is your favorite inside smell?

Buddy: Litter box.

Luke: What is your favorite outdoor smell?

Buddy: Everything.

Luke: Do you have to do any silly tricks to please your people? If so, what are they?

Buddy: I sit pretty to get a treat.

Luke: What kind of treats do you like?

Buddy: Bones from the meat market.

Luke: Do your people share their food with you?

Buddy: Yes.

Luke: What are your favorite toys?

Buddy: My doll Sally.

Luke: What is your pet peeve?

Buddy: Getting my ears cleaned.

Luke: Do you like other dogs?

Buddy: I tolerate them.

Luke: Do you like cats?

Buddy: Yes.

Luke: Do you listen when your people tell you to do something?

Buddy: Most of the time.

Luke: Do you have bad hair days?

Buddy: No.

Luke: Tell me about your family members.

Buddy: I love my mom and dad the most. I have two sisters — Bella and she is a yorkie poo and Bailey is a cat and one brother, Oliver who is also a cat.

Luke: Is there anything else you'd like to share?

Buddy: I lick my dad's feet every night before I go to bed.

Chubbs, the Book Dog

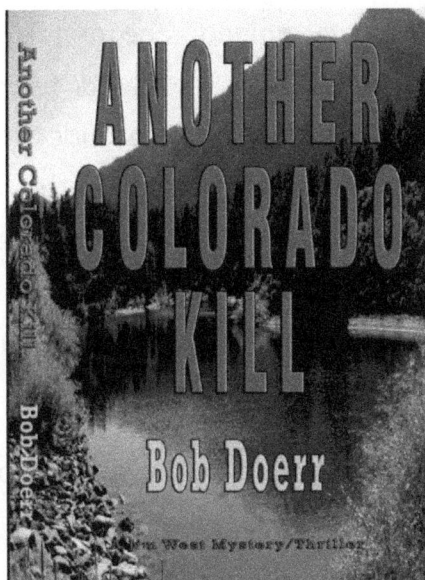

Figure 4   Chubbs' latest book

I'm Chubbs. I don't have a picture but I'm in this book!

Luke: Describe yourself.

Chubbs: I'm a forty-pound ball of black-and-white, wiry-haired energy. I've been told my mother was mostly a terrier who didn't run very fast. I also understand she never claimed any of the hounds around her neighborhood as my daddy, so no one's quite sure who he was. Jim, my owner, has told me I have a cocker spaniel face, but I'm not too sure about that.

Luke: I understand you're a book dog. Are you also a real-life dog like me?

Chubbs: I'm a book dog and proud to be one. The advantage of being a book dog is that more people get to enjoy your company.

Luke: What do you do in the books?

Chubbs: My main role in the books is to help make our house a home. I try to bring some companionship and "spice" into Jim's life. I don't know if you know this, but he went through a divorce that really devastated him a few years back.

Luke: Who is your book master? What is he like?

Chubbs: Well, I guess I have beaten around the bush. Let me tell you about Jim. He's approximately six, maybe seven years old — that's doggie years by the way. I don't know how to do people years. He's got light-colored hair, but not as white as that prissy poodle across the street. Jim's has a little grey in it. I try to keep him in shape and I think I've been doing a good job. I have to tell you, though, when I first met him, he was really down in the dumps. He looked like someone had run off with his favorite chew toy. He talks to me a lot when we're together, and I finally figured out that his wife had left him. Over the last couple of years though, I think he's getting back to normal. I worry about him when he goes away on those trips. He came back one time all banged up. Jim had more bandages on him than that collie down the road after the German shepherd caught him flirting with his girl friend. Jim's on a golf outing right now, but he's overdue. I'm worried again.

Luke: What are your likes and dislikes? Can dogs in a book smell?

Chubbs: Of course book dogs in a book can smell. That's why Jim bathes me now and then. And I can smell things, especially when I'm hungry and Jim brings me home something from the restaurant.

Luke: Do you think authors can successfully write about a dog's character?

Chubbs: I think authors can effectively write about dogs in their books, as long as they've been trained by dogs in their own lives.

Luke: Do you help solve the crime in your books?

Chubbs: I haven't had to solve any crimes in the books — yet. But, I'm willing to try!

Luke: Are you on the cover of any of the books?

Chubbs: I'm not on the cover of any books, but I understand the author has had the gall to put his own dog on the back cover of his newest book. I guess, like they say, it's who you know.

Luke: What do you like most about being a character in a book?

Chubbs: I like being the positive character in the book. I like being the reason Jim knows he has a home. Maybe he'll find another mate one day, but for now, there's just me.

Luke: What is your role when the book is being written?

Chubbs: My role in the books is pretty much what I've already said. I add another dimension to Jim's character and help give him a place he can call home.

Author Bob Doerr reports: "I modeled Chubbs after the dog my family had when I grew up. He was a mix of a mix of dogs, but we believed he was mostly terrier. I don't have a picture of him right now, but have attached the cover of my new book, *Another Colorado Kill.*

Joy, the Police Dog

Figure 5   Joy

Luke: Joy works for her living. She's a police dog and she helps get bad guys. Wow, I do that in the mysteries that Mom writes.

Luke: Tell me about yourself, Joy.

Joy: I am a Dutch shepherd. I was born in Holland and I speak Dutch as well as English and dog talk. I know that many people won't understand that I speak those languages but you understand, don't you, Luke?

Luke: Yep, I sure do. Dutch shepherds are smart dogs. Do you need to be smart to be a police dog?

Joy: Yes, there's a lot to learn. You don't have to be a Dutch shepherd to be a police dog but as a breed, we're smart, fast, and strong. It's a good combination for police work. We also have an exceptional sense of smell.

Luke: What exactly do you do?

Joy: I'm trained mostly to track drugs. I've learned the smells of different drugs and chemicals and I track them. My partner gives me the smell he wants me to follow and I take it from there. I put my nose to the ground, work as fast as I can and lead him to the drugs and the bad guys. Sometimes we track for a long distance. If it gets too long, we will probably lose the smell somewhere.

Luke: What do you do when you're not tracking?

Joy: If I'm working, I watch my partner and wait for him to give me a job. It's important that I do exactly what he tells me. That's what makes the difference between a good police dog and a mediocre one. Attention, intelligence, obedience, and courage — those are the important things in my job. I get excited thinking about my next assignment.

Luke: What's your favorite part of your work?

Joy: Catching the bad guys that are making or selling the drugs. When we find the drugs, my partner tells me to run to that spot and secure it. I love that part. It makes me feel like a hero.

I can hold a person or an object with my mouth but I never bite down unless my partner tells me to. He jokes that my reward is biting bad guys but the truth is that I don't really bite them. I scare them into thinking I will and that keeps them under control.

Luke: Where do you live and do you have a family?

Joy: I live with my partner. His family is my family. He has a wife and two kids. To relax, we play catch in the back yard. When we are in the house, I sit by him. The kids are little and I've been taught to be careful around them. I don't want to hurt them.

Luke: What is your favorite food?

Joy: I only eat one kind of food. I'm not sure of the name of it, but it is a healthy dog food that will keep me strong and alert. I eat once a day and only what I need. It's important that I stay lean and athletic.

Luke: What are your favorite treats?

Joy: I don't get treats. Since I'm a working police dog, I have to stay in good shape and I can't get distracted by treats. I only eat when my partner feeds me. I can never take food from anyone else.

Luke: I can't imagine what life would be without treats. I admire you, Joy.

Joy: Thanks, Luke. I think you're doing important work too. People need to know what dogs think about. I think our intelligence and love will amaze them.

Lois Thompson

Figure 6   Lois Thompson

Luke: I know you're a teacup Yorkie. Please describe your personality.

Lois: I'm happy...always. My family calls me "happy time."

Luke: What is your favorite activity?

Lois: Being with my mom...or my dad if mom is traveling.

Luke: What is your favorite inside smell?

Lois: Mom's lotion.

Luke: What is your favorite outdoor smell?

Lois: My sister's poop...but I am good and only smell it :)

Luke: Do you have to do any silly tricks to please your people? If so, what are they?

Lois: Tricks are for kids!

Luke: What kind of treats do you like?

Lois: I like everything. It all makes me happy.

Luke: Do your people share their food with you?

Lois: My sister and I get ice cream sometimes. My sister is a scaredy cat so I get more...hee hee.

Luke: What are your favorite toys?

Lois: Dad has a yellow chickie at his house that I'm partial to.

Luke: Do you have a pet peeve?

Lois: Having my beard cleaned by my dad.

Luke: Do you like other dogs?

Lois: I do.

Luke: Do you like cats?

Lois: Not sure.

Luke: Do you listen when your people tell you to do something?

Lois: I am an excellent listener.

Luke: Do you have bad hair days?

Lois: Often...but I'm so cute people overlook it.

Luke: Tell me about your family members.

Lois: They rescued me and I adore them. I think they feel the same about me.

Luke: Is there anything else you'd like to share?

Lois: Did I mention that I still have a tail?

Lola Burke

Figure 7 Lola Burke

Luke: Describe yourself.

Lola: I'm very cautious....doorways scare me...but once I become your friend, I'm a friend for life.

Luke: What is your favorite activity?

Lola: Going to work with my dad every day!!

Luke: What is your favorite inside smell?

Lola: Kibble.

Luke: What is your favorite outdoor smell?

Lola: Bird poop...no licking, just smell.

Luke: Do you have to do any silly tricks to please your people? If so, what are they?

Lola: Absolutely not! I don't believe in tricks.

Luke: What kind of treats do you like?

Lola: Turkey-flavored bacon and peanut butter flavored biscuits.

Luke: Do your people share their food with you?

Lola: No. Well...maybe a little of ice cream on a hot summer day...but I'm afraid of the spoon.

Luke: What are your favorite toys?

Lola: Dad's socks.

Luke: What is your pet peeve?

Lola: Loudness.

Luke: Do you like other dogs?

Lola: My sister.

Luke: Do you like cats?

Lola: Not really.

Luke: Do you listen when your people tell you to do something?

Lola: Always.

Luke: Do you have bad hair days?

Lola: Never.

Luke: Tell me about your family members.

Lola: They love me very much.

Luke: Is there anything else you'd like to share?

Lola: Nope.

🐾

Meko

Figure 8   Meko

Luke: I went to Sandcastle Days on South Padre Island with Mom and Dad. I had to walk in the hot sun but I like the feel of sand in my paws. There are lots of good smells there too.

I met Meko. She got to ride in some kind of cart with wheels while I had to walk. Meko is an eight-year-old Pomeranian. She's coal black and has the coolest haircut. Mom and I really liked her looks. I liked her smell too but Mom just wanted to take her picture.

Something didn't go right with Mom's camera. A bright light went off and Meko's face has some white on it but I know she's really all black. I'm sorry I didn't get her email so I could interview her.

She did tell me that she has a great life and she really likes her family. She sent me a message on my blog too.

Meko: Thanks for posting my picture on your blog. I had a great time visiting with you and playing on the beach and hanging out with my mom and dad at South Padre Island. By the way, you need to get your mom and dad to buy you a car/stroller. It is the ultimate way to travel. Get them to buy you some doggles (dog goggles) and you will get multiple interviews and pictures. Take care and safe travel - Meko

Luke: I think Bubba Rodgers wears doggles. I need a pair. I wonder if they smell good.

Ophelia

Figure 9   Ophelia

Luke: Describe yourself.

Ophelia: I am a white Great Dane/Lab Mix. I have great eyesight and a keen sense of smell because I am deaf. My name is Ophelia but I am called snorty, sneezy, yawnsey or goofy on occasion.

Luke: What is your favorite activity?

Ophelia: Sniffing, snorting, and sneezing. Anything involving my nose.

Luke: What is your favorite inside smell?

Ophelia: Bacon cooking or my food bowl being filled.

Luke: What is your favorite outdoor smell?

Ophelia: Other dogs.

Luke: Do you have to do any silly tricks to please your people? If so, what are they?

Ophelia: Laying down and rolling over — not necessarily in that order. I also put up with my dad who is constantly taking pictures of me.

Luke: What kind of treats do you like?

Ophelia: Milk bones.

Luke: Do your people share their food with you?

Ophelia: Absolutely not — although I get bacon leftovers in my bowl sometimes. My people are on a diet and have to watch their portions.

Luke: What are your favorite toys?

Ophelia: Any bones and I do not like to share.

Luke: What is your pet peeve?

Ophelia: I am not allowed on the couch, but guest dogs are allowed because they are spoiled.

Luke: Do you like other dogs?

Ophelia: I am the "Will Rogers" of dogs. Never met a dog I did not like.

Luke: Do you like cats?

Ophelia: Yes, but they do not understand that.

Luke: Do you listen when your people tell you to do something?

Ophelia: No, because I am deaf, but I watch their goofy gestures. I realize I have to play their game to get what I want.

Luke: Do you have bad hair days?

Ophelia: Never had one.

Luke: Tell me about your family members.

Ophelia: I have two people. They think I am adorable but they have a lot of rules. No furniture, lying down before mealtime, and sitting before I enter or leave the house.

Luke: Is there anything else you'd like to share?

Ophelia: I am smarter than my people — that is for sure.

Peanut

Figure 10 Peanut

I thought it would be fun to interview my sister, Peanut. She's a little bitty thing and I think I drive her nuts. I don't think she understand that I just want to play!

Luke: Describe yourself.

Peanut: I'm a beautiful but fragile chocolate teacup poodle. To tell the truth, I'm really nervous about life because when you weigh three pounds, everything in the world is big.

Luke: What is your favorite activity?

Peanut: Sleeping. I love to curl up in a little bitty ball.

Luke: What is your favorite inside smell?

Peanut: Treats.

Luke: What is your favorite outdoor smell?

Peanut: Other dog smells. I have to check if it's safe for me to be outside. If I smell another dog, I get really nervous and keep a constant look-out.

Luke: Do you have to do any silly tricks to please Mom and Dad?

Peanut: My mom and dad tried to teach me some tricks but why bother? They give me everything I want because I'm so little. They think I'm the cutest thing they've ever seen.

Luke: What kind of treats do you like?

Peanut: Soft ones. My teeth aren't very good. The vet says it's because I'm so small.

Luke: Do your people share their food with you?

Peanut: They used to. Now they sometimes give me a taste. I don't care to hang around waiting anymore. I know they'll take care of me.

Luke: What are your favorite toys?

Peanut: I don't play with toys. That's for kids. I'm nine-years-old.

Luke: What is your pet peeve?

Peanut: You, Luke. Mom and Dad said they wanted to bring a little brother home for me. You were supposed to be company but all you do is roughhouse and run around making silly noises. You need to calm down. I'm a senior now and I deserve respect. Another thing, you're way too big for me!

Luke: Do you like other dogs?

Peanut: Not really. They all want to smell me. I don't like that. Big dogs aren't as bad as middle-sized dogs. Of course, all dogs are big when you're little like me.

Luke: Do you like cats?

Peanut: Better than dogs. They usually leave me alone.

Luke: Do you listen when Mom and Dad tell you to do something?

Peanut: I used to. Now I figure I don't have to. Mom and Dad know what I want. If they don't do what I want, I stare at them until they catch on. Sometimes it takes forever! It would be so much easier if we spoke the same language.

Luke: Do you have bad hair days?

Peanut: Oh my, yes! Especially my ears. They are long. When I scratch them, I get them all matted. I hate it when Dad or the groomer tries to comb them out. I don't like the bows they put on my ears after my bath. I get them messed up and then they have to cut them out of my hair.

Luke: Tell me what you think about our family.

Peanut: It's you and me, and Mom and Dad. I liked it much better when it was just Mom, Dad and me. You create way too much havoc in our house. All in all, you're not a bad sort. You just need to cool it. I kind of like you when you're sleeping.

Luke: Well, I just asked a simple question. No need to make it personal.

Miss Prissy, is there anything else you'd like to share?

Peanut: I love to ride in the car! If I stand on Mom's knees, I can see outside. If you didn't always pounce on me, I would really enjoy it. I like to take walks once I get started but I'm usually not very motivated.

By the way, you do drive me nuts!

Luke: Geez, all I want you to do is play with me.

Rosie Faulkner

Figure 11   Rosie Faulkner

Luke: Describe yourself.

Rosie: I'm my Mama's baby girl, more commonly known as the curly girlie or the Little Red Poodle Dog. Everyone smiles at me and wants to pet me, and I like the attention, but my job is to watch out for my Mama. I understand English, but my Mama and Daddy aren't as good in Poodle so I have to SHOW them what they are supposed to do. <sigh> Do all cute doggies have such dumb Mamas and Daddies?

Luke: What is your favorite activity?

Rosie: I like to dance and sing. My favorite song is from RENT. I wanna go aooouuuuuut tonight! I do a good job with the aoooouuuuuut part.

Luke: What is your favorite inside smell?

Rosie: Daddy's breath after dinner.

Luke: What is your favorite outdoor smell?

Rosie: Daddy's breath before breakfast.

Luke: Do you have to do any silly tricks to please your people? If so, what are they?

Rosie: Well, I don't do silly tricks, but THEY do. You should see them dance & sing to get my attention.

Luke: What kind of treats do you like?

Rosie: Coooookies!

Luke: Do your people share their food with you?

Rosie: Do they have a choice?

Luke: What are your favorite toys?

Rosie: Plastic water bottles.

Luke: What is your pet peeve?

Rosie: When I want my Greenie and Daddy doesn't come give me one when I call him.

Luke: Do you like other dogs?

Rosie: Well, only for a quick sniff. I'm really a little fur person, you know.

Luke: Do you like cats?

Rosie: What cats?

Luke: Do you listen when your people tell you to do something?

Rosie: Sure. I listen and if it's something fun, I jump to it.

Luke: Do you have bad hair days?

Rosie: Oh no, I'm always gorgeous…even the week before I go see DeeAnn the groomer when I go into my Wookie Look.

Luke: Tell me about your family members.

Rosie: My Mama sings to me and I sing back. Every night, I sit beside my Daddy and put my paws on his chest and look deep into his eyes — and then at the bag of treats until he FINALLY gets the point and gets me a Deer Chewie.

Luke: Is there anything else you'd like to share?

Rosie: Got any cheese?

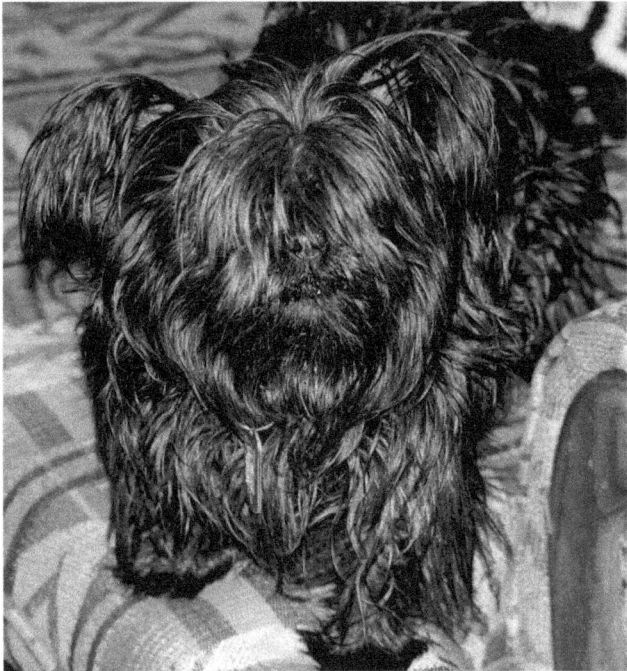

Spookie

Figure 12 Spookie Harless

Luke: Please describe yourself.

Spookie: I am a small Affenpinscher, sometimes referred to as a "Monkey Dog." I weigh approximately ten pounds. (When I eat a lot and don't exercise — sometimes I tip the scale at eleven pounds). I am probably the blackest dog you will ever see. My hair is coarse and shaggy — if cut it doesn't grow back, at least not very quickly.

Luke: What is your favorite activity?

Spookie: Chasing squirrels. I spent an hour one day trying to catch a squirrel. He would come down the tree within reach and as soon as I got there he went back up the tree. One time he came all the way to the ground and immediately ran up another tree before I could catch him. Then he jumped to a little building and then to the ground and ran under a trailer. I finally caught that squirrel and shook him good for teasing me. Then I tossed him in the air. When he landed, he got away from me again. I haven't seen that squirrel since.

Luke: What is your favorite inside smell?

Spookie: Raw hamburger. No matter what room I'm in, it draws me to the kitchen.

Luke: What is your favorite outdoor smell?

Spookie: Cow pie. I love to roll in it. My family tells me I stink, and they immediately give me a bath. (Not my favorite activity).

Luke: Do you have to do any silly tricks to please your humans? If so, what are they?

Spookie: Sometimes. They ask me to get a specific toy from my toy box and bring it to them. Once they get it they toss it away and tell me to "fetch." I don't understand why they ask me to bring it to them and then just toss it away. I generally humor them and take the toy to them. Sometimes I get stubborn and won't take the toy all the way back.

Luke: What kind of treats do you like?

Spookie: My favorite treats are Wagon Train Jerky Tenders. I like the duck better than the chicken. They call these my "Good Girl" treats. When I first came to my new home I sometimes made a mess in the house. They started giving me these treats after I would do my "business" outside. Now they give them to me only after I eat my dog food. I would do almost anything for one of these treats.

Luke: Do your humans share their food with you?

Spookie: Yes, sometimes they mix it with my dog food to get me to eat all the dog food and sometimes they feed me bites from the table.

Luke: What are your favorite toys?

Spookie: I like toys that squeak or grunt. At first my favorite toy was a monkey that made a strange jungle sound. I wonder if I was drawn to that toy because it is a monkey. The "Affen" part of my name is German for Monkey. Recently I have developed a special liking for my furry hedgehog. I have a difficult time making it grunt. Maybe I like the challenge. I like to roll it across the floor with my nose. It is almost as big as I am.

Luke: Do you like other dogs?

Spookie: I like small dogs, but big ones frighten me. However, I chase home the two big Shelties that sometimes come across the road. When I was little I used to play with the cutest little white dog. She looked like a little cotton ball. We visit her in Indiana about once a year. She occasionally travels to visit me. She is my best dog friend.

Luke: Do you like cats?

Spookie: No, I don't have any use for cats. When the neighbors' cats come over I chase them home.

Luke: Do you listen when your humans tell you to do something?

Spookie: I only listen if I feel like it. Sometimes I can be very stubborn and simply refuse to do what they ask. I will come when they whistle for me most of the time. There is a two-story old school house on our property. I love to go upstairs and often refuse to come down when they call me. It has all sorts of wonderful noises and sounds that make me want to just stay upstairs. I think squirrels occasionally get in the attic and make the sounds. Maybe I don't like to come down because I'm still a little afraid of coming down the spiral staircase. Going up is a breeze, but coming down is downright scary.

Luke: Do you enjoy going places with your human family?

Spookie: I love car trips. The only thing I don't like is being left in the truck when they grocery shop, or go in a restaurant to eat. When the weather's hot they don't take me as often. When they do they leave the air conditioning running to keep me cool. I really enjoy the long vacation trips. I have a special pillow between the driver's seat and the passenger seat. I spend a lot of time sleeping there. If they stop at a fast food place they always get me my own order. Sometimes I snore so loud that when I wake up I hear them laughing at me. They aren't very happy when occasionally I pass foul-smelling gas.

Luke: Do you have bad days?

Spookie: Yes, from time to time. It generally begins when the UPS man or the mail lady pulls in the driveway. I will bark and bark and bark. Anyone who knocks on the door will get a good loud barking from me. It really makes me mad when someone tries to take my toys or my food away from me. I sure sound ferocious then. I really wouldn't bite their hand, but I make them think I will. Generally they will leave me alone.

Luke: Tell me about your family.

Spookie: My dad is Mr. Paul and my mom is Ms. Ev.

Mr. Paul likes to tease me, but he also takes a lot of time to play with me. In the afternoon, when he lays down on the couch for a mid-day nap, he lets me curl up beside him for my nap. Ms. Ev says I snore louder than he does. Mr. Paul spends a lot of time restoring old jeeps. He lets me ride in them in parades and convoys.

Ms. Ev takes me for a walk each morning. We walk about a mile. I try hard to do as she asks. I don't bark at the cows, the horses, or the geese that sometimes swim in the pond. She likes to take pictures and wouldn't like it if I scared off the animals. She is the one who feeds, bathes, and takes care of me.

They are both retired and so have time to spend with me. I must admit though, I am a little on the jealous side. If Ms. Ev hugs or kisses Mr. Paul, I don't like it one bit. It is worse if a visitor tries to hug either of them. I jump up and down and bark like crazy. I generally sleep at the foot of their bed. Mr. Paul almost always goes to bed first. I like to stretch out on Ms. Ev's side of the bed. When Ms. Ev tries to get in bed

I bark and bark until Mr. Paul makes me go to the foot of the bed.

Luke: Sounds like you have a good life. Is there anything else you'd like to share?

Spookie: One of my favorite pastimes is watching TV. I especially like the wild animal programs. If it is suppertime I go in and get a bite of food and then go back to the living room to eat it while I watch the animals. Sometimes I try to chase them away by barking. Once in a while that works. I know every dog commercial. No matter what room I'm in I run to the living room to watch the commercial and bark until the dogs go away.

❖

Sweetie

Figure 13

I've never interviewed a cat so I had a hard time coming up with the questions. Like I told you, the only cat I know doesn't want me around but I figure there have to be good, friendly cats in the world.

My mom and dad know Sweetie's parents. They all agreed that I should interview her and make her part of this book. So...here's a cat's viewpoint.

Figure 14

Luke: First and foremost, do you like dogs?

Sweetie: Well, it's been quite a long time since I've been face-to-face with a canine. When I was just a fearless kitten, I didn't mind them so much. I am open-minded since I know my mom and dad have reunited several over the years with their people. So, they must be cool.

Luke: Please describe yourself.

Sweetie: Besides adorable, I wear several colors in my fur coat including black, white and gold. Everyone that I meet compliments me on my furry coat which feels as soft as a bunny. I like bunnies so that doesn't bother me. My mom and dad tell me that I'm very special because I only have one eye and three legs. My missing parts don't bother me. I can see fine with my one green eye and

I hop around the house like my bunny friends who live outside. I wasn't born this way. Somehow when I was very little, my back right leg and right eye were badly injured. The good news is that some nice people at the local humane society rescued me and an animal hospital fixed me up. Some people call me a pirate because there is a patch of black fur where my eye was removed. I also have a special tail that curls to help me balance since my one leg is missing. I'm very mature and I will be nine-years-old on March 28. I'm kind of famous because my mom and dad started a special emergency medical fund through our local humane society. They named it after me to help raise money so that other animals get a second chance when they are hurt.

Luke: Would you let a dog get close enough to smell you?

Sweetie: I would consider it a compliment if they wanted to smell me since I have a sweet natural kitty scent. However, it would be polite if they would ask first before sniffing.

Luke: Oops, guess I need to learn that "be polite" and "ask first" stuff.

Do you like to smell things as much as dogs do?

Sweetie: I like to check out what my two feline sisters and brother have been up to from time to time and smelling helps me figure that out. Cooking smells also interest me, especially when chicken or fish are on the menu.

Luke: Why do cats act conceited?

Sweetie: All I know is that everyone has always told me that I'm the sweetest and best kitty cat. Does that make me conceited?

Luke: Why does your hair stick up straight when you're mad?

Sweetie: First of all, I really don't get mad. I just might need to show someone who is boss from time to time. My hair may stick up when I get spooked after my kitty brother sneaks up on me.

Luke: Why doesn't cat food smell the same as dog food?

Sweetie: My mom and dad don't have dog food around the house so I'm not really sure if it smells the same. I just know from TV commercials that when I see the food dogs eat, it sure looks tasty to me.

Luke: Do cats have friends?

Sweetie: Yes. I would consider my feline sisters and brother my friends. I don't go outside so I don't go for walks to meet new friends. However, there are some kitty cats that hang around our house on the other side of our windows and doors. I just haven't been able to get to know any of them. Also, I don't have a Facebook page yet, but I'm quite sure that I would be very popular. My mom is always telling stories about me to all her friends and they always want to meet me.

Luke: You should get your own Facebook page. It's really cool and then we could check up on each other. Another question. Do you like humans?

Sweetie: I love my human parents! I'm a little shy when their friends come over but I do like humans. Some of my favorite humans are veterinarians which may be surprising. However, they're the best because they gave me a second chance at life when I was a little kitten.

Luke: Why don't cats have to obey humans like dogs do?

Sweetie: My humans take very good care of me. I get just about everything I want without obeying them — so, my strategy is working.

Luke: Why do humans put a dog on a leash but not cats?

Sweetie: Dogs need a little more direction and training than cats. We like to show humans the direction to go and don't need a leash to do so.

I tried a leash once but it's not comfortable. Besides, I rarely go outside and if I do, I prefer to be held.

Luke: I have to learn silly tricks to please my family. Do you?

Sweetie: When I was a kitten, my mom and dad used to throw furry mice toys and I would retrieve them. I was very particular and only would retrieve the green colored mice.

Luke: What do you do for fun?

Sweetie: I find time to play but not as much compared to when I was younger. To sharpen my hunting skills, I chase after furry mice toys to make my mom and dad happy. I just don't retrieve them anymore.

Luke: Do you think you and I could ever play together and be friends?

Sweetie: You are quite handsome so I would definitely consider hanging out with you for a play date.

Luke: Yippee! I knew I wanted to talk to a cat. I wonder if all cats think I'm handsome. Ooh, that compliment is going straight to my head.

Back to the business at hand. Tell me about your family.

Sweetie: My mom and dad are awesome because they really love animals, especially kitty cats. They have rescued many cats and dogs over the years and are very loving. I have an older feline calico sister, Sammy. She is fifteen-years-old, likes to nap a lot and not be bothered by us. I also have a younger feline tortoiseshell sister, Sissy who is seven-years old. She's my buddy and we hang out when she's not sleeping. Then there's the baby of the family, Sidney at one and a half years old, all black and very playful. He's a cool cat and watches out for all of us. He almost seems like a dog, herding us around alot. We have all been adopted and live inside the house.

Luke: Thank you, Sweetie. I'm really glad you're part of my first book. I think you're cool, very brave and fun too.

Vince Mathers

Figure 15 Vince Mathers

Luke: Describe yourself.

Vince: I'm Vince and I'm four months old. I weigh about 50 pounds now, and Mom says I'm still growing and full of the business, whatever that means.

Luke: What is your favorite activity?

Vince: I really like to chase my sister Greta, she gets mad at me and tries to run away, but I can catch her. I didn't used to be able to, but I can now. I also really like to go to work with Mom. She works with old people, but says I'm not suppose to call them old, I should say elderly or seniors, but whatever. They give me lots of treats and hugs, and always say I am really smart and cute. I try to be good while I am there, but someday I am going to sneak in their kitchen. It smells so good in there, but they won't let me go in there, because I might drop a hair or a germ or something. Someday though, when no one is looking, I'm gonna sneak in there and grab a BBQ chicken leg or maybe a hamburger.

Luke: What is your favorite inside smell?

Vince: BBQ chicken and hamburgers, and my mom. In the morning, she smells like fresh flowers and cupcakes, but later in the day she smells like a dog. And I love dog smell.

Luke: What is your favorite outdoor smell?

Vince: Birds. I love birds. I like to watch them land in my yard, and then chase them. In the morning, I can always tell that some bird has been in my yard, I can smell 'em. They have no business in my yard. Dang birds.

Luke: Do you have to do any silly tricks to please your people? If so, what are they?

Vince: Well, Mom says because I'm still a baby I only have to do what she tells me to and she just makes me do the usual for now. You know, sit, come when called, and lay down. But I have one thing that makes her laugh and I learned it all by myself. When Mom throws the ball for Greta, Greta runs to the end of the yard and brings it back. But if I catch Greta just before she gets to Mom, I can take the ball away from Greta and get it to Mom, and then I get all the praise because I was the one who returned it to her. Greta is so dumb. She lets me take the ball and get the praise, heeheehee.

Luke: What kind of treats do you like?

Vince: I guess I like dehydrated yams. Mom's a vegetarian.

Luke: Do your people share their food with you?

Vince: Sometimes. Mom is very careful about what we get to have. She says no onions, no raisins or grapes, and no chocolate. But we do get carrots and I love carrots. Oh and apples. Specially the apples that fall off the neighbor's tree. Yum Yum. My brother Chance will bark at the tree and that makes the apples fall off so we all get some. Chance is very smart.

Luke: What are your favorite toys?

Vince: Greta wrecked all my toys. I used to have some really cool stuffed toys and she tore them apart to get the squeakers out.

See how dumb she is. She thought there was a bird in there or something. She doesn't like birds either.

Luke: What is your pet peeve?

Vince: I'm too young to know what that means. But if it means things I hate, well I have been keeping a list. I hate it when other dogs get tied up outside, I feel bad because I know how much I like being with my family and I know they would like that too. I also hate it when on the news I hear another animal was hurt by a human. That just makes me so mad. No one has a right to harm another living being, even that I know and I am only four months old.

Luke: Do you like other dogs?

Vince: I love 'em, I mean what's not to love about dogs. They are smarter than people are, usually cuter than people are, smell better, and are more fun. Dogs are always ready to go for a walk or a swim or do whatever. They are sensitive and helpful and make great friends. You can always trust a dog.

Luke: Do you like cats?

Vince: Oh yes. Cats are so cool. When I grow up I want to be just like a cat. They get whatever they want and don't have to do any stupid tricks.

Luke: Do you listen when your people tell you to do something?

Vince: Of course. Well most of the time. Ok sometimes. But this is my childhood and

Mom says I am only a puppy once so I can get away with it for a little while. But I think I better start listening better. Mom isn't looking too pleased when I chase in the other direction when she calls. I have to go to puppy class to learn some manners and how to be a good dog. But that's all part of being part of the family, right?

Luke: Do you have bad hair days?

Vince: Never. My hair is just perfect. I am black and white, and have a big black spot on my side shaped like the perfect heart. Mom used to have another dog whose name was Charlotte who was just like me but she got cancer and died. Mom says this heart is a sign from Charlotte sending her love. I think it's because I love the Green Bay Packers.

Did I tell you I am named after Vince Lombardi? Yep, me, Vince.

Luke: Tell me about your family members.

Vince: Okay, there is Mom, who I just love and she loves me too. I can tell because she always smiles at me and tells me I am going to President someday. And there is dumb Greta. Mom says Greta is really very smart, but I don't see it. Chance also lives with us. I think he is Mom's favorite, because he has been here the longest. She calls him her little Chancey Pants. Whatever that means. Chance doesn't like me too much, he growls at me and never wants to play, and he absolutely will never share his toys, his treats, or even his bed with me. I don't know what his problem is. Mom says Chance is the best dog in the world, so I better watch him and learn what it takes to get that status. Best dog in the world — just wait till I get bigger, I will be the best dog in the world.

Luke: Is there anything else you'd like to share?

Vince: Yes. I would like to get serious for a minute. Mom says that too many animals are abused every year by the people who promised to love and care for them. We animals can't speak but if we could we would say "Please, please stop doing that! We are only here to make your lives better, so please stop hurting us." Oh and one more thing, always remember, if there ever comes a time, Vote for Vince.

🐾

Zoee Stockinger

Figure 16 Zoee with new sweater

Zoee is still a puppy but she has already learned some important facts about life with her new friend, MM.

Luke: What is your very favorite thing about MM?

Zoee: She feeds me, I'm pretty independent and I do like to stay close to her when she is home...and I make her laugh with all my antics and believe me I do some of the crazies, but most of the time she "gets" it.

Luke: Have you picked out some favorite smells yet? If so, what are your favorite smells — inside and out?

Zoee: Outside smell is other dogs peeing around trees, our deck and trees. Inside smell...food any kind.

Luke: What are the most fun things you and MM do together?

Zoee: I love it when MM goes and sits outside with me for hours and sometimes we play and sometimes I play and she reads. I hate to go in the yard alone, even to go potty.

Luke: What do you do all day while she's at work? Do you get lonely?

Zoee: I play with my toys and nap. I am desperately lonely and I HATE IT WITH MY WHOLE HEART. I know when she is leaving me already on Sunday Evening ... I pout, look sad, walk slow ... just plain droopy.

Luke: What is your favorite toy?

Zoee: Charlie — a white stuffed dog that looks like me and you and I got him for

Christmas. I carry him everywhere I go and then I chew him and shake him and abuse him, but he is my pal.

Figure 17 Zoee with Charlie

Luke: What is your favorite treat?

Zoee: I love those Cheese Pizza Treats the best.

Luke: Do you listen when MM gives you directions?

Zoee: Absolutely not! I love to please MM, but if I want to do something I will take the consequence. It's a catch twenty-two and if she upsets me, there will be a payback.... I may rip up a potty pad and spread it all over my room, or I may go doobers in the house, or I'll tear up the toilet paper or I literally look around to find what is gonna upset her.

Luke: Do you have MM trained yet?

Zoee: Nope...she is very strong and so am I and I think in some ways we really compromise. I know that it is very important to MM that I do not lose my spirit. She loves it when I am mischievous but when she flips cause I've gone too far....I run with my tail between my legs. I know I'm doing wrong while I'm doing it and sometimes I go get MM and show her and then I wait for whatever she is gonna dish out.....Now that is one of the dumber things I do...but I do it all time....

Luke: Do you like other dogs?

Zoee: I haven't had much interaction with other dogs. I'm an only child.

Luke: Where do you sleep at night?

Zoee: I have a space that has been created for me that is perfect, so I can play all night. I can go into my crate if I choose to. I have water and potty pads that I use to go potty at night so I am fortunate to have plenty of moving around space, but then I have my safe spot within the crate also.

Luke: Do you have to do any special tricks to make MM happy?

Zoee: I must sit and wait until MM gives me permission to eat...sometimes it is awhile, but this has helped me to slow down some. I also must sit before I can enter the house and I am learning to stay when she says to, but if something trips my trigger....I go on my poochie way and we start over.

Luke: Wow, after this interview, I knew that Zoee is a cool puppy and will be a fun — loving dog when she grows up.

Zoee has her own Facebook page, According to Zoee. You can follow her adventures as she grows up.

Me

Luke the Detective Dog

Figure 18 Luke

That's the last of the current interviews. I hope you've enjoyed meeting my dog (and cat) friends. The more I ask questions, the more I want to answer them myself. Since it's my book, I think I'm going to do just that. After all, you need to get to know me a little better

****

Describe yourself.

Me: I'm a handsome, all-grown-up Bichon. I'm white but I guess all Bichons are. Mom says I'm full of vim and vinegar. I don't even know what vim or vinegar is.

What is your favorite activity?

Me: Smelling just about anything or roaring through the house with my bone in my mouth. I love to drop it and pick it up as I run by. I'm pretty good at it too.

What is your favorite inside smell?

Me: My sister, Peanut

What is your favorite outdoor smell?

Me: Poop of any kind and other dogs.

Do you have to do any silly tricks to please your people? If so, what are they?

Me: Like I told you earlier, I have to patty cake for my mom. Other than that, she's pretty good at playing tug of war with me. I love to put my rope under my paws, play like I'm not paying any attention, and then nail her when she grabs for it. I'm pretty fast. I make her laugh a lot.

What kind of treats do you like?

Me: Dad is my main treat source. I like anything that's got flavor or that I can chew on: chicken treats, Snausages, stuff like that.

Do your people share their food with you?

Me: They play this silly game they call "last bite." If I don't disturb them when they eat, they save some crumbs for me — that is it, too — crumbs. The best days are when they're not hungry or don't like their food too well — then I get more. If it's something they love, I'm gonna go hungry.

What are your favorite toys?

Me: Wow, a hard choice. I like squeaky toys, bones and my rope. I love to carry stuff around. I hide my bones all over the house.

What is your pet peeve?

Me: Being ignored. I'm a friendly sort of guy and I expect people and other critters to be the same.

Do you like other dogs?

Me: Sure, I like them all, even the grumpy ones.

Do you like cats?

Me: I only know one and he's a nasty-tempered sort. I haven't met Sweetie in person but she sounds nice. Maybe she'll change my opinion.

Do you listen when your people tell you to do something?

Me: I listen but that doesn't mean I do it. Actually I don't listen if I'm thinking of something else or sniffing something really interesting. Mom says I'm single-minded. But I always listen when they say "treat."

Do you have bad hair days?

Me: Every day has its moments. Dad combs me every morning. I must have bad hair because he's always pulling it this way and that.

Tell me about your family members.

Me: There's Mom and Dad. They spend time playing with their toys every day. Then there's my sister and she's a little bitty thing. She's scared of me and she's boring. She doesn't even want me to smell her. I love her smell but she's touchy about it. She sleeps most of the time. I think she's old.

Is there anything else you'd like to share?

Me: I love my morning walks, running as hard and fast as I can, riding in a car or a golf cart, licking the car window, hanging my head out and getting tummy rubs. Most of all, I love it when anybody is paying attention to me. Life is good if you have a family and friends.

Oh, by the way, if you'd like me to interview you, contact me through my Facebook page: Luke the Detective Dog.

This is Luke the Detective Dog's first book but he is a character in Pat's fiction titles.

Luke's blog: www.lukethedetectivedog.com

Like Luke on Facebook:

www.facebook.com/lukethedetectivedog

Other Titles by Pat McGrath Avery

Colors of Kindness (e-book edition)

Fiction

Murder is for the Birds (First Place in Book Category, 2011 Association of Great Lakes Outdoor Writers)

Murder Takes a Ride

Non-Fiction

Emergence: The Story of Cinematographer John Bax (2012 publication)

The Sharon Rogers Band: Laughed Together, Cried Together, Crashed & Almost Died Together

They Came Home: Korean War POWs

Co-authored with Joyce Faulkner

Role Call: Women's Voices (Gold Medal, 2011 Stars & Flags Book Awards)

Sunchon Tunnel Massacre Survivors (Gold Medal, 2010 Stars & Flags Book Awards)